How to Potty Train a Puppy... in 7 Days or Less!

• The Best Beginner's Guide to House Training Your Pup Quickly and Easily •

By Dennis Mitchell

Table of Contents

Introduction 5

The Importance of Patience 7

The Natural Instinct of a Pup 9

The Benefits of Early Training 13

The Traits of a Strong Pack Leader 16

    Consistency 17

    Command 18

    Empathy 19

    Calm 20

The Power of Positive Reinforcement 21

How Often Does a Puppy Pee? 25

What Age is Best for House Breaking? 27

Can You House Break An Adult Dog? 29

Should You Use Treats to Potty Train? 31

Using Discipline Rather Than Punishment 33

Handling Accident Sites 37

Introducing the Crate 39

Choosing the Right Crate 44

Introducing Your Pup to His Crate 48

The Crate Outside the Home 52

Establishing an Eating Routine 54

Training Your Dog on a Leash 57

Is Paper Training a Good Idea? 60

Selecting a Designated Potty Spot 63

Seven Days of Potty Spot Training 66

My Dog is Still Having Accidents… 73

Welcome to Your Lifelong Friendship 80

Special Thanks 82

Introduction

The first time dog owner tends to be thoroughly surprised by the amount of work that it takes to turn a bundle of yipping fluff into a faithful companion for you and your family. When that little wet nose, those big puppy eyes and the oversized paws first trot into your living room, tail wagging wildly, it's easy to underestimate just how much work you've let yourself in for.

A puppy isn't much different from a new baby in those first few days. After all, your new pet is a baby themselves and has not yet had the life experience to know how to do anything at all, let alone pee in the right place and leave your slippers alone.

If you are not prepared for the experience of training your new puppy, it really is going to come as a shock. On the other hand, as any experienced dog owner can tell you, the effort you put in during this initial week will pay dividends for all the years of your dog's life.

Yes, you are about to experience days of chasing a wiggly ball of fur around the house and nights of whining and lost sleep. Yes, you are going to need to exercise all your diligence and innate parenting skills to teach this animal what its humans expect of it. And yes, it's occasionally going to feel like this is your life now – the effort is never going to end.

But the reality is that your puppy will learn extremely quickly compared to the long road of learning a human has to walk. It won't be long at all before your new dog has mastered its own bladder and knows what to do when it gets full, and all the little accidents along the way are a distant, slightly unpleasant memory.

This book will help you prepare for that first experience, so that you can tackle it the right way from the minute you open the front door and let your new best friend run through. No hiccups along the way, no misunderstandings and no need for either you or your pup to suffer through the process.

It might not seem like the most fun part of owning a dog, but you might be surprised how much bonding has taken place by the time your pup has been house trained – and at the sheer satisfaction you will feel in knowing you helped this little life take its first steps to adulthood.

So steel yourself and get the pup crate ready – the week ahead is going to need all your patience and supervision skills. The week after that? Well, that's just going to be the beginning of the most beautiful friendship you can imagine.

The Importance of Patience

Before you begin making plans to house train your new dog, it's very important that you get yourself in the right mindset to go about this properly. We have a tendency to think about the projects we take on from our own perspective, but in this case there is a second perspective to bear in mind – and it's more important than yours.

Your pup is a living, breathing, thinking animal, but he is also very, very little. Most pups are ready to come home at around eight weeks to three months in age, depending on the breed and the breeder; at that point, he is very much still a baby.

Human babies might be among the slowest learners of all the species on this planet (it takes us over a year to even figure out how to walk!), but that doesn't mean other animals are born knowing exactly how to get along in life. Your puppy is going to need to learn everything about his new world from scratch, and it's up to you to guide him.

There is a tendency for people who have never owned a dog before to forget this simple fact. Dogs, for the most part, are an extremely well behaved species, so we can easily fall into the trap of expecting them to behave perfectly right from the start.

This leads to inevitable misunderstandings. During this training process, your pup is probably going to whine a lot, be "naughty" and fail to understand what you are saying. If you're thinking of your dog as an obedient animal who knows what's expected of him, then you're obviously going to suspect you've invested in a badly behaved dog who is never going to do as he is told.

This is why it's so important to remember you are dealing with a baby. Just like a human, your dog needs to be guided right from the start – before those bad habits settle in – and treated with patience. Your puppy wants to please you and he wants to do what you are asking of him, but he doesn't necessarily know what it is you want – or how to do it.

Patience is the single most important ingredient to successful training. Your anger and frustration will negatively impact your efforts to train your dog, because it will leave him confused, stressed and unhappy. That's the perfect recipe for behavior problems in the future, so it's the last thing you want to encourage right now.

The good news is that, even though your new friend is still very young, he has arrived with a predisposition to be house trained. The ingredients are already there, so it will be your job to bring them together.

The Natural Instinct of a Pup

Just like humans are born with the instinct to breathe, eat and look for their mother, puppies are born with natural instincts already baked into their minds. You're going to want to know about these, because they are going to make the week ahead a whole lot easier than it could have been.

In particular, your puppy was born with a natural desire to relieve himself outside his own den and a second natural desire to please you, his owner. Your training is going to make use of both these instincts, because house training a dog is really all about tapping in to what the pup already knows and encouraging him to follow those instincts.

If your pup had been born in the wild, he would have started out both eating and eliminating his waste inside his den. Among his first experiences would have been his mother cleaning him almost immediately to get rid of the smell of waste.

As he got a little bigger and was able to move around on his own, at around four to five weeks when his sensory and motor abilities began to kick in, his mother would begin to care for him less intensively and, instead, would have gently pushed him outside every time he indicated a need to relieve himself. Pretty quickly, he would have learned not to make a mess on his own bed. In fact, at around five weeks old, when puppies have become able to pee and poop without stimulation, they will automatically seek a spot away from their den to relieve themselves

As he continued to grow, he would have moved further and further away from the den to poop and pee, because that's what his mother would do. He would have learned that the scent of his feces and urine can attract other animals, including predators, so it's better to leave those smells in a place that does not threaten his pack.

It's for this reason that dogs have evolved to be among the cleaner mammals on the planet. Your dog has a natural inclination to keep his sleeping, eating and pooping areas completely separate – he even prefers to play in a different area to the rest of these activities.

You can still see this behavior in action in your dog's closest cousin in the wild: the wolf. Though the pups we welcome into our home have been bred through the centuries to represent different sizes, shapes and personalities, and they lack much of the hunting for food instinct they once possessed, they all still maintain that same natural instinct to be clean.

This brings us to the second natural trait that will very much work in your favor as you begin to train your pup. Canines are animals who live in packs, which means they think in terms of leadership and their own place in a particular hierarchy.

Your dog expects there to be an alpha animal: a leader who dictates where he goes, what he does and how he behaves. If no alpha is present, he will automatically attempt to take on that role himself. This, obviously, is not an ideal situation in your home.

Not only can it lead to behavior problems as your dog tries to fill the alpha role and tell you how to behave, it can also lead to personality problems if your dog is not a born alpha and cannot fill the role with confidence. You will sometimes come across dogs who are trying to be the alpha because they perceive they need to take charge – they tend to be the ones that bark incessantly, nip at their humans and jump up at strangers in a way that can be either annoying (if it's a little guy) or threatening (if it's a big dog). As you can see, you neither want your dog to be good at being an alpha nor bad at being an alpha, so the only solution is to take on that position yourself.

Clear leadership makes your dog feel comfortable and at home. It also gives him confidence that he is doing the right thing, because he prefers to follow rules that have been defined by his pack leader.

A person who has been around dogs for a while comes to understand this pack mentality and acts on it without a second thought, so don't worry if it seems a little strange. Don't feel uncomfortable stepping into the role of pack leader, because in human terms that really only means taking on the position of "owner" or "puppy parent".

The two instincts your dog came into this world with are going to help you train him with a lot less effort than you might think. All you need do is try to think as your dog does and consider how he is interpreting the world around him, rather than how you yourself are seeing things.

House training a dog involves bringing together those two instincts by taking the place of your pup's mother. You are going to lead him out of the den and teach him that pooping and peeing are not things we do in the same place we sleep and eat, and he is going to instinctively grasp what you are telling him.

The Benefits of Early Training

When you first bring a puppy home, it's tempting to ignore the need to train him at first. All of a sudden, there's an adorable bundle of tail wags racing around your living room and all you want to do is play with him, pet him and swoop him into your arms for a snuggle.

It's hard to stress strongly enough that his training needs to begin immediately. You will have a happier pup and a better relationship, not to mention an easier time with dog ownership, if you begin this process as quickly as possible.

House breaking your dog is not just about making sure you don't accidentally step in something disgusting that your new friend left behind the sofa. That's obviously a big part of it, but there's a lot more going on here behind the scenes.

In the last chapter, we talked about the instincts we are going to be tapping into to train your pup to relieve himself in the yard, rather than on your bedroom rug. One of those two instincts was pack mentality.

House breaking is as much about teaching your dog his place within your pack as it is about teaching him where to pee. The ultimate goal is to train him to see you as pack leader, which will have the knock on effect of making him feel safe and calm within his new den and comfortable to follow your commands.

It's about setting rules and boundaries that your dog will be willing to follow. If he sees you as pack leader, he will easily submit to your commands. This, in turn, means you will be able to set rules for other behaviors more easily; for example, he will learn not to chew on chair legs if his pack leader has indicated this is unacceptable and he will follow your lead when reacting to guests.

When you see a well behaved dog, it's easy to assume the owner did a good job of teaching them to obey specific commands given with specific words. That's not really the case. Actually, the owner has done a great job taking the role of pack leader and has established rules for the dog that they are eager to follow, because following the rules of the alpha is what's best for the pack.

Your pup does not know or understand that he is not a wild animal, so as far as he is concerned it is just as vital to his wellbeing that the pack functions successfully as it would be if your family lived in the wilderness. Talking about life "in the wild" is really only a way to help us, as humans, understand a dog's way of thinking – to your new best friend, "in the wild" is a daily reality.

Your dog knows that his pack is his source of food, security, care and social interaction – it's how he's going to survive. He wants you to be a consistent, fair and considerate pack leader because that will help him understand his own place in the hierarchy and what you require of him. He needs a stable, stress free atmosphere to do this properly, which is why he needs you to set expectations and enforce them consistently. Most behavior problems in dogs are a product of insecurity; if your pup does not know what is expected of him, he will be confused and stressed and will likely do all the things you don't want him to do.

So please do resist that temptation to put training off until tomorrow, or the next day. You will reap the rewards of well-performed and consistent training for the rest of your dog's years, in every aspect of your relationship.

The Traits of a Strong Pack Leader

If you are going to take on the role of an alpha, you are going to need to know what that is. Particularly in these early stages, while your dog is getting to know you and is evaluating you as their pack leader, you must display certain qualities at all times when dealing with your pup.

Consistency

This is hands down the most important factor in successfully training your dog and taking on your role as his alpha. Your dog needs to learn what is expected of him, and part of that is learning what to expect from you if he does, or does not, follow your rules.

For a puppy, consistency also means that it's a good idea to set up a routine and then follow it doggedly. He needs to know there is a set time for eating, walking, going potty, even playing. If these activities follow a repetitive pattern he can understand and come to expect, he will feel secure that you, as his pack leader, have everything under control.

This will make it easier for him to follow the rules you are establishing. He will not be confused by an ever changing daily pattern and he will know exactly what the repercussions are if he misbehaves.

Command

How you take charge as pack leader is incredibly important. This one is quite easy to understand just by putting yourself in your puppy's shoes.

It's a similar relationship to the one you have or have had with a teacher, a manager or a boss. In that situation, they are fulfilling the position of pack leader and you are the pup trying to follow their commands.

A good manager knows that bullying, shrieking and anger are not great ways to get the best out of an employee. Rather, a manager should be firm but calm, should look you directly in the eye and should make firm decisions that are communicated clearly.

Getting angry with your pup, striking him when he has an accident and being unreasonable in your expectations is not going to get you very far. If you've left your dog at home for the whole afternoon and come back to find he's made a mess on the carpet, your job as pack leader is to understand that you set an unreasonable expectation that his bladder could hold for that long and that punishing him is not going to teach him better behavior.

Empathy

Your pup has only just arrived in your home, but it's not going to be long before his personality begins to shine through. It's your job to pay careful attention as this happens, because your dog's character is going to play a huge role in your relationship with him.

Keep an eye on his behavior to figure out his traits. Is he cautious when introduced to new things? Is he surprised by loud noises? Does he love to meet new people and go to new places?

Just like a human manager can help an employee flourish in their role by understanding their talents and limitations, you will get the very best out of your dog by understanding his personality and working with it, rather than against it. Not only will your dog be happier if he can act in a way that feels natural to him, he will respond better to his pack leader if his routine and expectations are easy for him to follow.

Calm

It cannot be stressed strongly enough that the last thing you could ever want is for your dog to fear you. An assertive, dominant dog will react to this emotion by fighting back, while a less dominant dog will cower and become miserable.

Your job as pack leader is, first and foremost, to provide your dog with a sense of confidence in his own behavior. He needs to feel he is doing the right thing, because his natural instinct is always to do the best possible thing for his pack.

Your dog needs to respect you, yes, but that comes from displaying the traits we've discussed in this chapter. Physical punishments, raised voices and other unhealthy forms of dominance will only serve to make your dog feel fearful and lead him to believe he cannot trust you, which will damage your relationship and lead to bad behaviors as he acts with uncertainty instead of confidence.

The Power of Positive Reinforcement

In the last chapter, we touched on the idea of giving your dog confidence by establishing dominance through calm and consistent commands. Let's look a little closer at how this impacts your training methods.

Specifically, let's consider the question of whether it's better to reward your puppy when he does the right thing or punish him when he does the wrong thing. Each of us naturally swings towards one or the other of these teaching methods, so which one will work better when house breaking a dog?

It's an easy answer that you've almost certainly guessed already. Your puppy will flourish if you use positive reinforcement to train him.

When you praise your pup, you assure him that he is doing the right thing and pleasing his pack leader, which is what he naturally wants to do. When he trots outside and relieves himself in the yard, letting him know this was exactly what you wanted him to do not only reinforces his natural instinct, but helps him understand he is correctly following his alpha's rules. It's also, of course, much more pleasant to be rewarded than punished, whether you're a human or a pup.

Looking at it more closely, you can clearly see why this would be the case. If you smack your dog when he gnaws on a cushion, shout at him when he poops on the welcome mat and yank the leash when he pulls on it, your dog will come to expect pain and fear as a result of his behavior. He will begin to worry about your potential reaction and will be unsure how to proceed.

If you praise your dog when he pees in the right place, give him kind words when he comes to you when you call and pet him when he plays nicely, he will seek more of those pleasant rewards. He will be even more eager to please you than his natural inclinations dictate, and your relationship with him will deepen.

Dogs function best when there is routine and consistency, and they will look for these things and attempt to establish them. When you reward your pup for a particular behavior, your positive reinforcement is filed away in his brain and he will continue to follow that pattern.

Can you still use negative reinforcement while in the process of training? Yes, it can still be helpful if dome mindfully. In a lot of cases, it will be a better idea to completely ignore accidents and moments of bad behavior – dogs are clever animals and will quickly work out that they prefer to do the thing that will get them a reward to the thing that won't get them anything at all.

It's also important to understand that, while your pup is an intelligent creature, he doesn't have human levels of reasoning. If you find a poop on the kitchen floor and react by telling your dog off and being displeased, there's a good chance he won't have any idea what's made you mad because he's clean forgotten pooping there in the first place. Even if he can see the poop, he may not associate your reaction with the creation of that poop, which may well have happened a long time ago in puppy minutes.

If you come across your dog in the act of relieving himself in the wrong place, it's absolutely fine to firmly say "no" to remind him of the rules and immediately take him to an acceptable place where he can finish off his business. (As a side note, don't underestimate how well a dog can read your body language – if you let it show in your stance and facial expression that you are annoyed, he will absolutely be able to tell!)

Once he's done, reward him with a positive reaction and a ruffle of his fur – you'll be surprised how quickly he makes the connection that peeing in the wrong place is against the rules, while peeing in the right place gets him a reaction that makes his tail wag.

Your pup prefers it when you praise him – that's the reaction he desires and will instinctively aim to achieve. Never underestimate the power of making your puppy feel good for doing the right thing; just like a human, he will want that pleasant feeling to happen again as much as possible.

It's your job to make him earn that praise, which is something he will instinctively understand. He will learn more quickly than you might imagine what behaviors will get him pets, treats and praise, and those are the behaviors he will be more inclined to repeat.

How Often Does a Puppy Pee?

You know a lot about puppy psychology at this point, but what about puppy physiology? A basic understanding of when and how often your puppy needs to relieve himself can also be incredibly valuable during this training period. If you know when he needs to go, it's a whole lot easier to make sure he's going in the right place every time.

Well, the first thing to know is that your dog will likely wish to urinate as soon as they wake up in the mornings, and after a nap (particularly when they are young). Some like to poop after sleeping, too.

Most dogs will also need to poop around 20 to 30 minutes after they have eaten.

As for how big a puppy bladder is: not very big at all, at least at first. The general rule of thumb to follow is that your dog will be able to hold his pee for as many hours as he is months old plus one; so, for example, he can hold it for two hours when he is one month old and six hours when he is five months old.

But how long he can hold it and how long he should hold it are different things. While your pup is in training, and until he is six months old, you should be taking him to his designated pee spot every one to two hours in the daytime.

At night time, he will need to go to his bathroom at least once during the sleeping hours until he is around four months old. It's a good idea to set your alarm to take him outside around five hours after his last pee during this time.

What Age is Best for House Breaking?

There is a sweet spot for house breaking, according to the best research on dog behavior. The very best time to embark on this project and strengthen the bonds between you and your new best friend is when he is between six and eight weeks of age.

This will form your bond early, which will have the positive effect of making your dog more willing and eager to please his pack leader and more attentive to other training you wish to give him.

It's also recommended that a dog be separated from his mother and siblings and placed in his new, loving home at around seven to eight weeks of age, which is when he will be more inclined to join his new pack and form an attachment to you as his owner and alpha.

Potty training will ideally begin as soon as your pup comes home with you and will likely take a couple of months. The average dog is house broken by four months old, but don't be disheartened if that's not the case with your own furry friend. Every dog is different, and some will take a little longer to learn new habits than others. As long as the training is consistent and appears to be proceeding according to plan, there's no need to worry if it's taking extra time. Don't change what you are doing or try to speed up the process – he will get there, eventually, if you are faithful to your plan.

Speaking of expectations, it's not a good idea to expect miracles from your pup before they reach the age of 16 weeks, because he simply can't control the relevant muscles yet. It's important to know that the time between a young dog feeling the need to pee or poop and the actual act happening (with or without their consent) is much shorter than it will be when your dog is an adult.

A couple of months of the recommended potty training period falls in this time when your dog does not yet have full control. That's why it's going to be your job to learn his "tells" – the movements and sounds he makes when he feels that urge – and immediately respond to them.

Some dogs will turn in circles, others will sniff the floor, some will go over to the door and push their head against it, others will whine. Learn how your dog indicates he's feeling the need to potty as quickly as you can and take him straight outside to the place you would like his to fulfill that urge. Remember that everything you do at this time in your dog's life is a potential learning experience, and your dog is constantly looking to learn.

Can You House Break An Adult Dog?

There's an old saying that everyone knows and believes: you can't teach an old dog new tricks. If you have dismissed the idea of adopting an older dog or visiting an animal shelter to rescue your pup because it will be far too late to train him to fit into your family, please do think again, because that saying is frankly poppycock.

All dogs have the capacity to learn new things, just as all humans can pick up a new skill if they so choose. The only real difference is that you may not be able to tell if your dog has undergone potty training in the past or is coming to this project completely fresh.

It's easy to give in to the temptation to purchase a dog from a reputable breeder, who will have begun potty training and other socialization and will present you with an animal who is primed and ready for training. But please don't discount the rescue pups – it really won't be much harder to help them adapt.

It's true that even a dog who was house broken in his previous home may revert to older habits while in an animal shelter. Some shelters are pretty overcrowded with minimal volunteers to care for the animals, so it's possible he wasn't given as many opportunities as he needed to do his business outside and soiled his own kennel area a few times. This will have weakened the habits he learned through his training.

Meanwhile, the two of you still need to get to know one another. He will still need to accept you as his pack leader and you will need to learn what signals he gives when he needs to go potty.

The answer to this is simple: no matter where you find your pet and how old he is when you first meet, it's best to start your potty training as quickly as possible and keep it consistent until he has learned his new routine.

Should You Use Treats to Potty Train?

We've touched on the idea of positive reinforcement in this book already, but it's worth diving a little deeper into the power that praise has to bring about the training results you want. Let's also take a look at treats as a training tool – and why they aren't nearly so effective as a few kind words.

Especially as your dog gets used to their potty routine and you come to expect that they will get things right more often than not, it's easy to forget to praise them for something that has become a normal part of your day. But for your dog, that praise is both motivation and pleasure, and is a huge boost to his ego that will push him to do his best.

Particularly while he is a puppy, take advantage of his love of praise by making sure to show him that he has pleased you greatly every time he does something right. Be enthusiastic and free with your praise, both with your voice and in petting your pup as you tell him he's done well.

Treats are, of course, another way to express pleasure with your dog, and some people use them to motivate good behavior during the training period. This isn't something that we would recommend, however, because it can actually do more harm than good.

You don't really want your puppy to learn that doing his business will earn him a treat, partly because he'll be very interested indeed in these nuggets of delicious food and will be paying more attention to getting their teeth into the crunch of dog biscuit than he is to learning where and when to go potty.

The other issue is that treats as an incentive is not a sustainable method. Your dog is going to pee and poop multiple times per day for the rest of his life – you don't really want to be feeding him extra calories every time he does.

Not to mention that it really isn't necessary. Your dog actively wants to work hard to please you – he wants to know he's done well, so what he is really looking for is your praise. Reserve treats for the times you really need them, or don't attach them to any particular reward, rather than use them to help you with potty training.

Using Discipline Rather Than Punishment

There is a significant difference between the idea of using discipline to guide your dog and the concept of punishment, but many new puppy parents find it difficult to tell the difference. It's an instinctive reaction to tell your dog off when he does something wrong, because that's what we'd likely do when dealing with another human being, but it's not going to have the same effect because your dog reasons in a very different way.

Yes, it's true that your dog will learn to obey you if you shout or hit them when they make a mistake. It is indeed possible to train an animal not to relieve itself in the house using those tools. But you're not going to end up with the pet you were expecting to own.

The key fact to remember when training your dog is that praise causes an ego boost that will promote his ability to learn, while punishment causes a fear response that actively inhibits his ability to learn. In other words: while he is afraid, he is finding it much more difficult to learn what you want him to know because all his instincts have been diverted into protecting herself from apparent harm.

It makes sense if you think about it in human terms: if you were dangling over a precipice above a thousand foot drop, would you be able to concentrate properly on figuring out an algebra problem?

The knock on effect is that you will teach your dog to be wary of you. He will never trust your intentions when you reach for him because he will have learned that he cannot be sure whether you intend to hurt or pet. As you might imagine, this is something that is going to deeply affect your dog's personality.

That's not to say that you cannot use discipline as a tool, because it's a very different thing. But all you are ever going to need to discipline your dog is a single word: "No".

During the initial training period and likely for a few weeks after, it's normal for your puppy to make the odd mistake when going to the bathroom. It's a good idea to expect this to happen and see it as a teaching opportunity, because it's less likely to make you feel annoyed when it inevitably happens.

When accidents happen, discipline is possible. However, there is a caveat: discipline will ONLY work if applied while the dog is in the act of making a mistake. It will NOT work at any time after, because your dog will not be able to connect an earlier event with your current discipline.

If you see your dog squat down to pee while inside the house, follow these easy steps:

1. Immediately say "NO" loudly and firmly.
2. Clap, stamp your feet, rattle something or otherwise make some noise that will distract your pup from what he is doing. You want to startle the dog into stopping what he is doing rather than scare him.
3. Pick up the puppy and carry him outside (or pull him out by the collar if he's too big).
4. Allow the pup to do his business outside, in the appropriate place.
5. Praise the dog effusively as soon as he does.

Try to avoid taking any other actions when an accident occurs. If you didn't see it happen, it's important that you say nothing at all to the dog. When you catch him in the act, follow the steps to the letter. The reason for this is that you don't want to accidentally interrupt the pup's learning in other aspects.

For example, if you use the command "come" to have him come to you to receive discipline, he will associate that command with being told he did a bad thing. That's not good, because you want him to be willing to obey the command "come" instantly when you need him to return to your side in a hurry, which means he needs to associate it with positive experiences rather than discipline. As you can see, using it in this situation could mean he fails to return to your side later, when it's an emergency.

By following these steps, you teach the dog a very specific, and very helpful, lesson: when he pees in the house, he can expect to be disciplined, but when he pees outside, he gets praise.

Unsurprisingly, your dog will learn this lesson fast, because what he wants more than anything else is praise. He will greatly prefer to choose the action that gets him the praise over the action that does not, so this will go a long way towards your training efforts.

Handling Accident Sites

Those accidents that are so useful to your house breaking efforts? They also leave a mess, but the biggest problem with that mess has nothing to do with how disgusting it can be to clean up.

The issue with accident sites has to do with your dog's nose, which is a whole lot more sensitive than yours. The amount of cleaning that would make an accident site smell fresh and pure to a human nose is not enough to remove its smell for a dog.

The accident site needs to be deodorized as well as cleaned in order to completely remove the smell. If this is not done, your dog will still be able to catch the scent of urine or feces and will consider that site to be a bathroom.

Much of the time, this is what's going on when a puppy returns to the same place over and over again to have an accident. Dogs prefer to do their business in the precise place they did their business last time, or where another dog has peed. It's a way for them to mark their territory and also makes them feel safer.

Invest in some heavy duty home cleaning equipment – you'll likely need cleaners that can be used on carpet and sofa or bed material as well as on hard surfaces. Use these first, removing as much of the offending liquid as you possibly can, and follow with an odor remover that has been formulated to handle urine and feces. These are quite easy to find and are usually labeled as "pet stain" removers.

The ammonia in a dog's urine smells worse and worse the more it breaks down. At a certain stage of decay, mercaptans are produced, which smell even worse than the ammonia. If you catch a whiff of such odor somewhere in the house, it's likely come from an accident that was not completely cleaned and is in the process of decay.

If you're not sure where it's coming from, use a black light in a darkened room to locate it. Urine will glow under this light, which makes it a lot easier to find the problem area. A dog owner needs to be fastidious about these scents to prevent their pup from making the same mistakes over again.

Introducing the Crate

Earlier in the book, we talked about how a young dog would develop and learn if he was living in the wild and introduced the idea of a "den". One of the first things a puppy learns, once he has the motor skills to move around by himself, is that he doesn't want to soil himself in the same place he plans to sleep.

This concept is the key to successful potty training. We're going to teach your dog that your house is his den, and it's not a place for him to pee. We will start that lesson small and expand it from the tiny area his little body needs to sleep to include the entire building and every room within.

We're going to do that using a puppy crate. This will be his den, to begin with, and he will learn fast that it's not somewhere he wants to relieve himself. You will have the advantage of his natural instincts to teach him this lesson – in fact, it's not something he really needs to be taught at all. The training you will be doing over this first week is intended to reinforce the instincts nature has already provided.

The puppy crate is a small, confined area in which your new friend will sleep at night. He will feel safe and secure in his den, which is a good thing all of its own, and will avoid soiling it if at all possible.

Some pet owners feel concerned that "caging" the dog is cruel or will make it feel miserable. Don't worry, that's unlikely to be the pup's reaction. He knows you are nearby, so he won't feel separation anxiety, and the crate will make him feel protected rather than confined. Remember that dogs are naturally den animals and like to have a space that belongs to them alone, so they will be comforted to know that they can go to their cage at any time.

Remember also that your dog is not the alpha in this pack and will be happiest when he understands the rules he is meant to follow. The clearer the rules, the happier the dog, so the crate will help him establish what he is meant to be doing and feel more comfortable overall.

Another benefit of the crate is that it will teach your pup the valuable lesson of "holding" his pee when it's not possible for him to go outside. Obviously you don't want to make him hold it so long that he suffers, but it's still something he's going to need to know. When you go out for a while or are sleeping, your pup will not be able to relieve himself the second the urge arises, so he's going to need to understand that he can, and should, hold his pee until he can go outside. Because he won't want to make a mess of his den, he will start learning this lesson right away, while also developing his muscle control to be able to hold that pee in.

It's also a healthy way to train a pup because everyone feels more secure and less anxious – not just the pup! When your new pet can roam the house at will and is constantly disappearing out of view, you're going to worry what he's doing and spend half your time following him around to check he's not pooping or chewing on the cat. If, on the other hand, you know he is happy and in a safe place where he is less likely to have an accident or damage your belongings, you'll feel a whole lot calmer. And a calm owner is often the secret to a calm dog, because your pet can sense more of your emotions than you might think!

Your pup is going to rest and relax inside this crate whenever you leave the house, sleep or are otherwise not able to keep a close eye on him. It's not, and should never be used as, a place of confinement or punishment in any way. You want your dog to love his crate and see it as a place of safety, which isn't going to happen if he's sent there for doing something wrong.

Another mistake to avoid is keeping your pup in his crate for too much of the day. A new puppy is hard work, it's true, and nobody would blame you for wanting a break, but he can't stay in there constantly or he won't learn to expand his vision of what a "den" is to include the whole house – and he won't have much chance to bond with you and your family.

Unless you are genuinely unable to watch the puppy at this moment – because you are in the shower, leaving the house, sleeping or otherwise occupied – he should be outside the crate and subject to your commands and supervision. Whenever it starts to seem like you're getting nothing done except watching your puppy, remind yourself that this is a temporary thing, and it won't be long before he is a fully trained and valuable member of the family who will do the right thing whether you're keeping an eye on him or not.

Will you continue to use the crate once your puppy is completely house broken? Maybe, but maybe not. Some dogs love their crates so much that they will continue to return to them long after reaching adulthood and you may feel inclined to keep it around for your pet to make use of when he wishes. Other dogs will stop using their crates over time and will prefer to sleep on the sofa, on a dog bed or even on the human bed with you. If this is the case, you might still want to keep it around for times when you are out of the house for a long period, but it probably won't be necessary. In the end, the decision will be yours and will be based on your dog's preferences and needs.

The crate should be placed in the middle of your house, in as central a location as possible. It might seem more convenient to place it in a corner of a utility room, a garage or a lightly used area of the house, but you want your dog to understand that they are a member of the family and the entire house is a den, and therefore a place to keep clean.

The crate is the first bit of the house that your dog will learn to keep clean and the center point for your training efforts. Everything you do while he is outside the crate will be focused on expanding his definition of "den" to include the rest of the house, but the first step is to introduce the very idea of a den by using the crate.

Your first task, therefore, is to choose the right crate for your animal and the environment he's living in.

Choosing the Right Crate

When you visit the pet shop or browse online to find a dog crate, don't be surprised if you quickly feel completely overwhelmed. Because we love our animals, we've designed a startling array of potential dens for them – and each one will be a little bit different.

We can narrow things down right away by limiting our choices to either a plastic crate or a wire one. Ignore the plush crates, expensive styled ones and soft sided containers, at least for now. You are dealing with a young animal who is going to be very interested in chewing things when he starts teething, and he's not going to give two hoots how much they cost to buy. It's also a time in which accidents are a strong possibility, so you won't want to invest in something that's hard to clean.

Wire crates are an excellent choice if you live in a warmer climate, because they are better ventilated and stay cooler. This also makes them appropriate for dogs with thick coat and breeds that have short muzzles and can experience breathing problems.

Wire crates also have the advantage of a removable floor that can be taken out to clean, and they usually don't absorb odors. Some can be folded down for storage and transport.

However, you can't use a wire crate to store a dog for travel on a plane or train, which might be limiting for your lifestyle. They are also harder to move easily, so are not necessarily a good choice if you want to keep the crate in the living room during the day and move it into the bedroom at night.

Plastic crates, on the other hand, are lighter and easier to transport. Some dogs prefer them because they are more private and confined, which increases their sense of safety. One half can be stacked in the other for storage, while their structure makes them a little bit harder for dogs to break out of because their solid sides make it more difficult to get to the outside latch.

They do, however, get hotter because the air circulation is not as good as in a wire crate, while your animal will not be able to see much of their surroundings while inside. The lack of vision will suit some dogs and help them relax without distraction, but others may feel anxious and disconnected from the pack.

In terms of size, it's going to depend on the breed of dog you have chosen to bring home. A crate measuring 24 inches is perfect for a Chihuahua or pug, but you're going to need a 54-inch crate for a Great Dane or a St. Bernard.

This brings up an important question for the fiscally minded: what happens if you bring home a tiny Husky puppy who only needs a small crate to feel cozy and safe, but will be a hundred pound dog within a few months?

The key to crate size is that you want your dog to have enough room to lay down comfortably without feeling confined, but you also want the crate to be small enough that your pup would not be able to "escape" from an accident. A mistake new dog owners often make is to buy the crate their puppy will eventually grow into, rather than the crate that fits them now.

The problem with this is that your puppy can pee or poop at one end of the crate and then go back to sleep at the other end, without having to stay too close to their own waste for comfort. You want your dog to learn that relieving themselves in their den is uncomfortable and definitely not a good thing, which isn't going to happen if there are no consequences to having an accident.

The trouble, of course, is that these two things don't combine very well. If you are on a budget, you don't want to have to purchase several different crates as your puppy grows.

Fortunately, there is an answer: some crates, particularly wire ones, come with dividers. While your dog is still tiny, you can use this divider to limit the space available to him. As he grows, you can move it outwards to give him more space.

Before we continue, I have a small favor to ask:

Could you please take a minute of your time to write an honest review of the book?

Your reviews are what keeps me going. I read every single one of them, and would be **extremely thankful** if you choose to share your thoughts with me.

* * * * *

Introducing Your Pup to His Crate

You've chosen your crate and you're feeling pretty confident about this potty training thing, but the next step is going to be more vital than you might think. You can't simply put a dog in a crate and expect him to be happy about it. This needs to be a place he enjoys, feels comfortable in and is happy to spend time when you need him to.

Before the dog goes anywhere near the crate, turn it into a cozy place for him. Do this out of your pup's sight, particularly if you need to assemble the crate and that's going to involve some scary loud banging noises he won't much like.

Don't leave the crate bare once it's assembled. Place an old towel or blanket inside for him to curl up on and feel cozy. Buying a bed or mattress at this point could well be a complete waste of money because this is the time when accidents are most likely, and if he is at all anxious he may feel the need to chew.

Once the crate is ready, place it in the space you've chosen for it – preferably in the center of the house. Place a couple of treats in there and call your pup over. Make a big fuss of him and of the crate, praising him and petting him while he explores so he knows this crate is a good thing and that you, as his pack leader, are happy with it.

Let the pup explore the crate, trotting in and out and sniffing it. If he tries to wander away, call him back and encourage him to go inside it and look around.

This may take some time, depending on the temperament of your dog and whether there's something else going on in the house he considers more interesting.

When your pup seems to feel comfortable inside the crate, and has gotten used to wandering in and out on his own volition, gently shut the door behind him while he's inside. Don't make a fuss, or latch the door, just swing it closed. If and when he turns to sniff at it, open it back up again to get him used to the idea that the door is a temporary barrier.

Keep making use of praise during this process. Leave the door closed for longer and longer, following the same routine of opening it back up when he sniffs at it, until he seems content with the crate with the doors closed.

At this point, give the pup a bone or a toy to occupy him, close the door and move away from the crate. Keep an eye in case he gets distressed, because you don't want him to develop negative feelings about his new sleeping place – if he does, open the door back up and give him praise and pets to reassure him.

The next stage is to get him used to the idea of sleeping in this crate. Pups take plenty of naps, fortunately, so this can be done fairly quickly. Next time he falls asleep, pick him up and transfer him into the crate, but leave the door open so he can leave it when he wakes up.

This process shouldn't be too difficult. Don't forget that dogs have an instinctive desire for a den of their own, so you're working with his nature to give him exactly what he thinks he needs. As long as you accomplish this process without any negative feelings developing towards the crate, it shouldn't be problematic in the slightest.

Once he's happy with his crate, be sure to place it in an area and at an angle from which he can see what is going on if he needs to be there during the day while you are at home. He will not feel comfortable if he can't tell what is going on in his pack. At night, move it to your bedroom or close by the door, so he knows you are nearby.

If he makes a mess in his crate – which is a distinct possibility at first, it's incredibly important to remove him from the soiled area as quickly as possible and clean it thoroughly. Dogs are clean animals and he will not relish sitting in his own waste – it will likely make him feel less positive towards the crate. Remember that your dog should never, ever think of his den as a place of punishments. It's a refuge, so it should be clean and comfortable at all times.

A couple of notes: take your dog's collar off at all times while he is in the crate. It's all too easy for it to get caught and tangled and leave your pet trapped or injured, which is not only a natural thing to want to protect your beloved pet from, but is also going to be a negative experience associated with the crate.

 Finally, try not to disturb the dog while he is in his crate. Other pets, children and even adults should be encouraged to leave him in peace and quiet, because that's exactly what his crate – his den – should represent to him.

Now your pup has a den, you should be able to relax a little more at night and when you are outside the house. Please do remember that a small pup can't hold his bladder for as long as an adult dog, so you will still want to set your alarm at least once during the night to take him outside to relieve himself. If you have to leave him in the day, try not to leave him for longer than his bladder can comfortably hold.

The Crate Outside the Home

Your pup is not going to need to stay confined to his crate forever – this is a training tool, above all else. However, some dogs do continue to enjoy their crates into adulthood and there's no need to get rid of it when he grows up if you think he is still benefiting from its presence.

It's an even better idea to hang on to the crate if you travel a lot. Your pup's den will be a safe place for him in a strange new part of the world, which will keep him relaxed on his journeys.

Life does not stop just because there's a new pet in the house, of course, so let's focus on what the crate can do for you right now when you need to travel away from home. Your pup's den can have two functions in this situation: it will keep him content while you are on the road and it will make him feel safer and less likely to have an accident when you arrive.

If you need to take a road trip during your training time (and for several weeks after he's got the hang of potty training), place the dog in his crate while you are in the car. He will feel safer and happier and he will also know not to make a mess inside your vehicle, which until now has not been part of his extended den.

Whether you will be staying in a hotel room or at a friend or family member's house, you will be taking your pup into an unfamiliar environment. Not all dogs will feel anxious about this, but the crate will help to calm his nerves if he does.

More importantly, it will keep him from making messes in this unfamiliar place that is definitely not part of his den. At night and when you leave the room, you can use the crate to reassure him and at the same time remind him to hold his bladder until you get back.

Establishing an Eating Routine

By now, you are well aware of the importance of consistency in your dog's training. It might not have occurred to you, however, that there needs to be consistency at the other end of the line as well.

In other words, you will need to establish a routine for taking in food just as much as for then getting rid of its waste. Your dog needs regular, sensible eating habits from the moment he steps through your front door.

The reason for this is to encourage a steady appetite in your dog and help to regulate his digestive processes. It will help him get to know his own schedule – and it will help you do the same.

Select an appropriate dog food that is designed for your dog's stage of life. If he is a puppy, choose a food that has the correct nutrients for a growing dog. If you have brought home a rescue dog, choose one that will be appropriate to his age and breed.

The amount of food your pup needs is something that you will need to find out over time. Right now, you can't be sure how active he is, how the climate will affect his digestion and so on. Begin by following the recommended guidelines on the packaging and then adjust as necessary if your dog appears to be hungry or is putting on too much weight.

(Be aware that rescue animals can sometimes develop an anxiety reaction with food and will continue to eat long after they are actually hungry. If your dog spent time as a stray or was separated from his mother too early, he may have a different relationship with food to a dog who has always had access to regular meals. An animal who has learned that food can be scarce will always try to eat as much as possible in one sitting and will immediately begin looking for more. If your pup may fall into this category, his "hunger" may not be real and may not be the best indication when setting food quantities.)

Once you've chosen the food, picked the right time and purchased a dish for your dog to eat from, all you need do is follow this routine. Your pup does not need variety in his food or meal times – in fact, he will not relish this. He will find it comfortable to eat the same thing at the same time every day.

Give your pup around 20 minutes to finish his meal and then take any leftover food away. While some dogs do like to stretch their meals out for a lot longer – and some will take all day to finish a bowl – that's not a habit to encourage, especially during potty training. Remember that your dog will need to poop around 20 to 30 minutes after eating, even sooner when very young, so your goal is to establish a routine where he eats and is then taken to his potty spot at the same time and in the same manner every day.

If you do not set meal times in this manner, your dog will need to eliminate waste a lot more often. While you are trying to establish good habits, avoid giving human food or treats and keep his meal times to a sensible length, quickly followed by a potty break.

During the early stages, if your dog is under three months old, he will need to be fed four times a day, in the morning, at lunch time, in the late afternoon and in the evening. This can be reduced to three feedings between the ages of three and six months, two feedings from six months to a year and just one feeding when he reaches a year old (though large breeds may need two meals).

While you are house breaking the dog, it's also a good idea to limit his access to water. It's important that he gets to drink regularly, but this should be done on a schedule for the same reason that you will be feeding his on a schedule. Once he is house trained, a water bowl can be made available at all times for him to drink from at his own leisure.

Training Your Dog on a Leash

If you don't have a back yard or a fenced in area in which your pup can roam safely without fear he'll find a way to escape, you will need to train him to wear a collar and leash before you can begin training him to go outside to potty. Even if you have chosen to use puppy pads at first, you should begin this process as quickly as possible and before you start training him to do his business outside.

Begin by getting him used to wearing a collar, choosing a cheap but serviceable version that will fit his small neck. He's going to grow out of this collar, so there's not much point investing a lot of money.

When you first put the collar on your dog, don't be surprised if he reacts by wiggling and rolling and doing everything he can to get it back off. Stay with him, praising him constantly so he associates the collar with good things. If he is still fussing after around 15 minutes, remove the collar and let him run free.

Repeat this process a few times each day until he accepts the collar without complaint and stops attempting to remove it. Some dogs will be fine with a collar right away, others will take a while to get used to it.

When your dog is content with his collar, snap a leash onto it and let go. Don't hold on to the leash, let your dog wander around the house with it unhindered. Keep an eye, of course, because he's almost guaranteed to get the leash wound around six table legs and the cat's tail in the space of a single blink, but let him choose where he goes as he gets used to the sensation.

Next, take hold of the leash, but continue to allow the pup to take lead and go wherever he wants to go. Do this for a few sessions before you begin attempting to guide him in the direction you want him to go.

If he pulls, tries to rush ahead, rolls over or even turns and rushes behind you, squat down to his level and tell him to "come". You can gently tug the leash to encourage him, but be careful not to do this hard enough to hurt or frighten him. When he does come, administer a whole lot of praise, then walk forward with the leash in your hand.

Keep following this step until he has learned that he is supposed to walk beside you. Now you can try taking him outside.

If you live in a city and your only choice when taking your dog outside to pee and poop is the street, you want your dog to get used to the idea that he is supposed to go potty when outside. For this reason, you should only ever take him out for potty time during the seven day training stage and not for a long leisurely walk. There will be plenty of time for that later.

Is Paper Training a Good Idea?

You are no doubt aware that such a thing exists in your local pet store as a potty training pad for your dog. This works almost like a diaper in that it soaks up urine and holds feces, except that it can be laid flat on the floor for your pup to squat on.

Should you use this device? If possible, it should be avoided at all costs. The sooner you start taking your dog outside to pee, the sooner he will be house broken. Not to mention that these pads violate his natural instincts to avoid soiling his home and will make it more difficult for him to learn that the whole house counts as his den and is not for peeing or pooping in.

However, if your dog is extremely young and still in the stage at which he would not yet be leaving the den if he was living in the wild, it is ok to use these pads. You may also need to use them for a couple of days while you concentrate on leash training and getting him used to his den. If you can avoid doing this, you will benefit from having done so in the end.

If you do need to use a potty training pad, make sure to place it within your dog's crate or confinement area. Be sure there is no visible floor space within that area – there should be nothing but a sleeping mat and a potty mat.

This is the best way to use the pads to promote your dog's natural instinct to eliminate waste away from his bed. Most pads are scented to encourage the dog to use them, but you can also buy sprays to use on them if necessary. The scent is based around pheromones to attract him to the right spot – you can also use the spray during outside training if you want him to always use the same spot in the back yard.

Potty training pads do have their uses. Life brings unexpected challenges and you may find yourself responding to an emergency situation and having to leave the puppy at home, in which case he's going to need a place to do his business.

However, it is a bad idea to design your training schedule around what's easier for you. If you are in the middle of a very busy period, if you have responsibilities that will take your attention away from the pup or if you simply don't think you can handle the amount of effort this is going to take for the next week or two, a puppy might not be the right choice for your life. It's better to wait for a better time than it is to rely on a training mechanism that's less than ideal.

Don't forget this training period is temporary. It will be intensive for a week but will then grow easier quite literally by the day. Once you are done, if you have attended to his training properly, you will have a dog who is extremely low maintenance, happy and content for the rest of his days.

So by all means use the potty training pads, but please do limit them to emergency use and the first couple of days after your dog comes home with you, when you are training him to wear a leash and spend time in his crate. As soon as you have those two things done, start your outside potty training in earnest.

If you've picked up this book after the dog has already joined your family and you've been using the pads so far, don't worry – just stop using them. Dogs learn fast and they learn well, so it's pretty much never too late to begin proper house breaking with him.

Selecting a Designated Potty Spot

Once again, this part of your training is based on your dog's own natural instincts. He is a creature of habit and will be more than happy to fall into a routine that is given to him – in fact, he will flourish from the consistency.

Before you begin taking your dog outside regularly to do his business, select a spot in which you would like him to do most of his peeing and poops. It should be as far as possible from any areas of the yard that are used for walking and at a distance from your patio or any other heavily used area.

It shouldn't be too far from the house, of course, because this is a spot you and your dog will be heading to several times a day from here on out. Try to choose a relatively secluded corner, where your dog can have some privacy – many dogs feel anxious if they feel "watched" while they eliminate.

You are doing this firstly so that your dog confines his waste to one part of the yard, which means you are less likely to tread in an unexpected mess while trying to enjoy a walk through your yard. You are also doing this because your dog is quick to make associations.

In other words, your dog will learn very fast that his potty spot is a place to pee and poop. Heading for that spot will begin to trigger a reaction to eliminate, so you'll probably find that he will try to go potty there even if he doesn't need to go.

When you are in a hurry, you'll find this reaction a blessing. Dogs who have not been trained in this way can sometimes take many minutes of wandering in circles to decide where they want to go, which can be a pain if you need to leave the house or if the weather is bad.

Bear in mind when choosing the spot that this will always be your dog's potty spot. Once you've built that trigger reaction for him to relieve himself as soon as he reaches it, that's what he is always going to do. If you live in a part of the world where the weather gets bad in winter, this is something you'll want to bear in mind, because you're going to need to reach that spot even in the middle of a blizzard.

If possible, section off the potty spot with a small border fence to help your dog recognize where exactly his area begins and ends. It's also helpful for his human family members, who will know there's a danger zone inside the border for bare feet.

You are going to need to

If you do not have a yard, don't worry – you can still designate a spot on the street. Choose a lamp post or a hydrant or tree or bush and be consistent in taking your pup to that place. Try to choose a place that's relatively near your home, especially if there are stairs or an elevator between you and the potty spot.

Seven Days of Potty Spot Training

It's time to put everything you've done so far to work to potty train your pup in the next seven days. This guide assumes you will be home and available all day for this short but intensive period, or that you have a partner or house mate who can share the load while you are away. If that's not the case, don't worry – we'll talk about how to handle training on a busier schedule next.

• The night before training begins, take your dog outside to go potty and make sure he evacuates his bowels and bladder completely. Bring him back inside and place him in his crate for the night. By now, he should be content to stay in his den. Be sure it is near your bed so you can set your alarm to take him out again in the night, and so he feels comforted to know you are nearby.

• As you go to bed, place your shoes and a coat or dressing gown nearby. Set your own alarm for a specific time that is close to your usual time of waking up – you're going to be getting up consistently at exactly the same time every day while this training is taking place. Why at your normal waking time? Because you want your dog to learn to hold his bladder until you are awake, you should start out as you would like to carry on.

• When your alarm goes off, immediately get out of bed and slip on your shoes and gown. Do not delay to visit the bathroom yourself or for any other reason. Take the pup from his crate, place a leash on him if needed (because you are heading out to the street or a non confined space), carry him outside and take him directly to his potty spot.

• Put your pup down in his potty spot and wait quietly and patiently. Allow him to sniff around, find the spot he wants and prepare to eliminate. Sniffing is an important part of stimulating the need to do his business, so don't try to hurry him. Move around very slightly while you wait.

• While this is going on, choose a phrase that you will always use to direct your dog to do his business. "Go potty" or "go pee" or something similar works well – a short phrase you can remember is best. It doesn't matter what words you use, it's the sounds your dog will come to recognize, so what really matters is that you remember it and are consistent.

• When your dog has relieved himself, take some time to praise him and tell him what a great dog he is, then take him back indoors. Do not give him time to wander the yard and explore – he needs to associate outside time with going potty at this stage of his training.

• After a brief period of supervised play, it's time for the first meal of your pup's day. Put out his breakfast along with a bowl of water and give him 20 minutes to consume from both.

• When time is up, remove both bowls and put the leash back on the pup. While you do so, choose a second phrase that your dog will come to recognize as meaning he is about to be taken outside to go potty, such as "Let's go outside". You should try to use this phrase every time you go out to the potty spot so your pup learns to recognize it.

• Return to the potty spot and repeat steps four and five. If your pup pees or poops, praise him enthusiastically. If he does not (which is perfectly possible at this early stage of establishing a routine), take him back inside, place him in his crate and try again 15 minutes later. Repeat this until he does his business.

• Give the pup a little play time outside his crate, supervised by you, and then place him back in his confinement area until his next meal. Repeat steps seven through nine to feed him and then take him outside to go potty.

• Repeat steps seven through ten for the rest of the day: a period of play, a period of confinement, feeding time then potty time.

• Throughout the day, whenever your pup lays down to sleep, watch carefully for when he begins to wake up and take him outside immediately. He will almost always need to eliminate after a nap.

• As the week goes on, you should also be working on the amount of time your pup spends outside the crate. At first, he will likely only be able to cope with 15 minutes or so without having an accident. The goal is to extend this time slowly such that your pup will eventually only need to be confined when you are asleep or outside the home (and not at all when fully matured). If your dog gets very excited while playing outside the crate, take him outside for a potty break.

• Between potty times, keep a close eye on your puppy to spot any signs that he needs to relieve himself. His behavior will change, though exactly how it will change will depend on the specific dog. Watch for actions such as turning in circles, seeming restless or uncomfortable, sniffing and making noises. As soon as you see any behavior changes, take the pup outside, following the steps to encouraging him to go potty. Don't wait to be sure the signs are really what you think they are, because the time between the behavior change and the action of eliminating is very short for a young pup.

• End the day with a final visit to the potty spot before placing the pup in his crate for the night.

During this first period, you may be taking the dog out to his potty spot up to ten times per day, but this will likely halve as he settles into the routine you are working to establish. Make sure to be consistent in when and how you are feeding him and taking him outside and deal with any accidents as directed in an earlier chapter.

If you are dealing with an older dog, you won't need to take him out as often because his bladder will have matured, but the steps to follow will still be the same.

If you are unable to avoid going to work during this period, try to start the training at the weekend so he has a couple of days of full training before you must leave him for an extended period. When Monday comes, follow the steps above before you leave the house and after you return home. When you leave the house, do so without any fuss to alarm your pup and leave him feeling any more unhappy at your absence than necessary.

During the period you are away, establish a larger confinement area than you otherwise would with an area for him to relieve himself – he is going to need to do this, he will not be able to hold it all day long. Limit the amount of water you leave in his confinement area.

If possible, ask a friend or neighbor to visit the pup at least once during the day to follow the steps to feed him and take him to the potty spot.

Come straight home from work and make a huge fuss of your pup. Ignore any messes – they are inevitable with such long gaps between potty spot visits – and do not attempt to tell him off for his accidents. Not only will he not be able to understand what you are telling him off for because too much time has passed, it's not his fault his bladder is still too tiny to be left for a long period.

Take him outside immediately as you get home and then follow the training steps for the rest of the evening. Maintain as much consistency in your schedule as possible, including at the weekends when you are home.

By following this simple schedule, built on all the practical and mental preparation you have done ahead of time, you will be surprised how swiftly your dog becomes house broken. He's still very young, however, so accidents are still possible and you will need to continue being consistent throughout the next month or longer in terms of meal times, potty breaks and confinement.

After the seven days of intense training is over, you can relax a little in your routine to suit both you and your dog. He will now be ready to spend more time outside his den with you, his owner, and will have learned to keep his den clean and free from mess.

My Dog is Still Having Accidents...

If your potty training has been successful and your furry friend is doing his business consistently in the outdoors, you might feel disheartened to discover a stray puddle or pile inside the house.

Does this mean your training has not been successful and your dog is never going to learn what you expect of him? Absolutely not. There are plenty of reasons for your dog to have an accident inside the house, none of which are signs your training has been a bust.

Let's take a look at the possible reasons for his accident so you can figure out what happened (or what is still happening) and either ease your mind about your training or potentially remove the problem to make sure it stops happening:

Excitement: A young or old dog especially may lose control of his bladder when he gets very excited, or feels threatened. If your dog thinks he's going to be punished, is welcoming you home after a long absence (or an absence that feels long to him!) or is deeply involved in a play session, this may happen.

Too Much Time Alone: If you've had to leave the house for an extended period of time, especially if your pup did not relieve himself properly before you did, then it's possible he simply won't be able to hold it in until you get home. That's understandable – you probably couldn't hold it either, in the same circumstance! It's nothing to worry about in terms of training, just a simple fact of nature.

Medical Issues: It's possible that your pup has a bladder or urinary tract infection. If the peeing problem has come on quite suddenly and seems quite serious, check with your vet for any signs of a medical problem.

Territorial Marking: Did you recently bring home a new pet? Have the next door neighbors bought a new dog? If your pup feels his territory has been invaded, he may feel compelled to scent mark its boundaries with pee or poop. One sign that this is the cause of your pup's accidents will be the size of the accident: if it's pretty little, it may well be a territory issue.

Fear: Another reason for a dog to lose temporary control of their bladder is fear. This can be a bigger problem with rescue animals, who may have suffered adverse experiences in their past lives, but can happen with any puppy. Loud noises are a common culprit, so, if you find a mess, consider whether it has happened during a thunder storm or while someone nearby is shooting off fireworks.

Separation Anxiety: If you have to leave your pup home alone, be aware that he might become anxious about your absence. Some dogs find it more difficult than others to cope with being separated from you. The good news is that you can usually tell if this is the cause of a dog's accidents because there will be other signs of their anxiety, such as destructive behavior and howling. Solving separation anxiety requires training all of its own, but is most certainly a solvable problem.

Welcome to Your Lifelong Friendship

If you've followed the steps in this book and committed to them completely, and you've understood the theory of routine, consistency and natural instinct on which they were based, you may well be reading these final words with a happy pup laid by your side, content in your company while you feel relaxed in the knowledge you can trust him not to make a mess.

Congratulations! You've set yourselves up for a lifetime of companionship and love, with a firmly established relationship of respect and a routine that your dog is happy to follow.

It takes around 30 days for a pup to be completely housebroken, though it's only the first seven days that require constant attention and vigilance. However, on a final note, it's important to realize that your work is not completely done.

Now you've got the basics covered, you can work on increasing the size of the house he is allowed to roam in, the amount of time he stays outside his crate and, more importantly of all, his willingness to obey your commands as soon as they are given. Just because he is no longer making messes doesn't mean you can quit repeating your command words, following a potty spot routine and keeping an eye on his behavior.

You already know that this won't be nearly as difficult as you once thought it might be, and that the reward of watching a happy dog follow your commands is very much worth the effort. The hard part of your journey is over – the part where your best friend walks beside you and offers you unconditional love and endless joy has just begun.

Special Thanks

I would like to give special thanks to all the readers from around the globe who chose to share their kind and encouraging words with me.

Knowing even just one person found this book helpful means the world to me.

If you've benefited from this book at all, I would be honored to have you share your thoughts on it, so that others would get something valuable out of this book too.

Your reviews are the fuel for my writing soul, and I'd be **<u>forever grateful</u>** to see *your* review, too.

Thank you all!

Made in the USA
Monee, IL
10 July 2023

38941937R00046